MENU

of

CHOCOLATE

Edited by
Jeffrey Young & Angus Thirlwell

Author: Allegra Strategies
Contributor: Hotel Chocolat
Design: John Osborne
Researcher: Becky Hindley
Publisher: Allegra Publications Ltd

Dedicated to
Jenny, Damian, Natalie, Amanda and Sarah
&
Libby, Phoebe and Fergus

Today is a good day
to have a good day.

Life without chocolate
is a day without sunshine.

A good life is waking up
an hour early to live an
hour more.

The world is a safer place
once I've had my chocolate.

Chocolate is the answer. Who cares what the question is!

I put chocolate on the top of my to-do list today. That way at least I'll get one thing done.

Seven days without chocolate makes one weak.

Chocolate first,
schemes later.

I've never met a chocolate
I didn't like.

Chocolate doesn't ask
silly questions;
chocolate understands.

Life is like a roller coaster.

It has its ups and downs.

But it's your choice

to scream or enjoy the ride.

Always be a little kinder than necessary.

J. M. BARRIE

Coffee makes it possible
to get out of bed, but
chocolate makes
it worthwhile.

Cocoa. The food choice of warriors, adventurers and pleasure-seekers for centuries.

The question isn't who is going to let me; it's who is going to stop me.

AYN RAND

One kind word can change someone's entire day.

I was going to save this chocolate for a rainy day... It's raining somewhere isn't it?

Willy Wonka:
'Oh, you should never,
never doubt what nobody
is sure about.'

HILAIRE BELLOC

Chocolate is nature's way
of making up for Mondays.

There are four basic
food groups:
milk chocolate,
dark chocolate,
white chocolate
and chocolate truffles.

Hot chocolate is like a hug
from the inside.

There's nothing wrong
with me that a little
chocolate won't fix.

What on earth could be more luxurious than a sofa, a book and a bar of chocolate?

How you make others feel
about themselves says
a lot about you.

Chocolate – because
anger management
is too expensive.

Don't wait for the perfect moment. Take the moment and make it perfect.

The definition of good parenting: your children know to leave Mummy's chocolates alone or else.

I'd give up chocolate,
but I'm not a quitter.

When life gets you down,
just think about how
much better it is than
living without chocolate.

If life was easy,
where would all the
adventures be?

Chocolate might not make
the world go round.
But it certainly makes
the trip more worthwhile.

Never underestimate
the power of chocolate.

Giving chocolate to others
is an intimate form of
communication, a sharing
of deep, dark secrets.

MILTON ZELMAN

Don't spend your life with
someone you can live with,
spend it with someone
you can't live without.

Don't forget what happened
to the man who suddenly
got everything he always
wanted... He lived happily
ever after.

WILLY WONKA

I want someone to look
at me the way I look
at chocolate.

Save the Earth.
It's the only planet
with chocolate.

A chocolate a day
keeps the grumpy away.

Life is like a box of chocolates, you never know what you're gonna get.

FORREST GUMP

Life is short. Surround yourself with good people and great chocolate.

A balanced diet is
chocolate in both hands.

As long as there is chocolate in the world, how bad can life be?

One good piece
deserves another.

Chocolate – the other vitamin C.

Chocolate is health food
for the soul.

When I went to school,
they asked me what I wanted
to be when I grew up. I wrote
down 'happy'. They told me I
didn't understand the assignment,
and I told them they didn't
understand life.

JOHN LENNON

Be happy for this moment.
This moment is your life.

OMAR KHAYYAM

Coffee, cake and chocolate.
Like men, some things are
better rich.

Money may talk,
but chocolate sings.

Don't judge the path
you haven't walked.

Do we really need scientists to tell us there are benefits to eating dark chocolate?

Chocolate is cheaper than therapy and you don't need an appointment.

JILL SHALVIS

Good chocolate is a
pleasure, real friends
are a treasure.

My policy on chocolate
is pro having it and pro
eating it.

Never let the things you want make you forget the things you have.

Chocolate says 'I'm sorry'
so much better than words.

RACHEL VINCENT

Birthdays are good for your health. Studies show that people who have more birthdays live longer.

Chocolate, chocolate
and more chocolate,
need I say more.

When life gives you lemons, throw them back and demand chocolate.

You only live once,
but if you do it right,
once is enough.

MAE WEST

Chocolate –
a healthy passion.

Trifles make
the sum of life.

I've learned that people will forget what you said, people will forget what you did, but people will never forget how you made them feel.

MAYA ANGELOU

If 'Plan A' doesn't work,
the alphabet has 25
more letters!

CLAIRE COOK

I can give up chocolate.
I've done it many times.

'Nearly eleven o'clock,' said Pooh happily. 'You're just in time for a little smackerel of something.'

A.A. MILNE

Do you believe in love at first sight? Or should I walk past again?

Life happens,
chocolate helps.

Every accomplishment starts with the decision to try.

GAIL DEVERS

I love you more
than chocolate. But please
don't make me prove it.

Big things often happen
in the little moments.

You will always be
my favourite hello
and hardest goodbye.

CECELIA AHERN

When times are good
you want chocolate.
When times are bad
you need chocolate.

A day without you
is like a day without
chocolate.

I heard a theory that chocolate slows down the ageing process. It may not be right, but do I dare take the chance?

Kindness is like chocolate.
It awakens your spirit
and improves your day.

Give me chocolate to accept
the things I can change
and wine to accept the
things I cannot.

There is nothing better than a friend, unless it is a friend with chocolate.

LINDA GRAYSON

Have a heart that never hardens, and a temper that never tires, and a touch that never hurts.

CHARLES DICKENS

If music be the food of love, play on.

SHAKESPEARE

Strength is to break a chocolate bar into four pieces with your bare hands and then eat just one of those pieces.

A day punctuated with chocolate is a day well lived.

People who love to eat are always the best people.

JULIA CHILD

Everyone has a price.

Mine's chocolate.

Given enough chocolate,
I could rule the world.

If you want something
you've never had,
you have to do something
you've never done.

Good friends are like
a box of posh chocolates.
It's what's inside that
makes them special.

If a woman is upset, hold her and tell her how beautiful she is. If she starts to growl, retreat to a safe distance and throw chocolate at her.

If I have 10 chocolates
and someone asks me
for 1, how many chocolates
do I have left?
That's right, 10.

All you need is love.
But a little chocolate
now and then doesn't hurt.

CHARLES M. SCHULZ

I would rather die
of passion
than of boredom.

VINCENT VAN GOGH

The 12-step chocolate program: Never be more than 12 steps away from chocolate!

TERRY MOORE

There is no sincerer love than the love of food.

GEORGE BERNARD SHAW

You'll always be my friend.
You know too much.

Besides chocolate,
you are my favourite.

To eat is a necessity, but to eat intelligently is an art.

FRANÇOIS DE LA ROCHEFOUCAULD

Willy Wonka:
'A little nonsense
now and then
is relished by
the wisest men.'

ROALD DAHL

Life's short.
Buy the shoes.
Drink the wine.
Eat the chocolate.

It was like having a box of chocolates shut in the bedroom drawer. Until the box was empty, it occupied the mind too much.

GRAHAM GREENE

Never regret anything that makes you smile.

MARK TWAIN

Without chocolate, life is just a bunch of Thursdays strung together.

Me + Chocolate =
Forever Together.

No matter how you feel,
get up, dress up, show up,
and never give up.

Nothing goes better
with chocolate than
more chocolate.

Man cannot live on
chocolate alone,
but women sure can.

One cannot think well,
love well, sleep well,
if one has not dined well.

VIRGINIA WOOLF

Promise me anything but give me chocolate.

Publicity is nice,
but chocolate would
be better.

You can never start a
new chapter of your life if
you keep re-reading
the last one.

TGIFC –
Thank God I Found
Chocolate.

I tried to be good,
but there were too many
other options.

Research tells us 14 out of
any 10 individuals
like chocolate.

Never look down on anybody unless you're helping them up.

JESSE JACKSON

Thanks for the chocolate.
But what are you going
to eat?

What you see before you,
my friend, is the result of
a lifetime of chocolate.

KATHARINE HEPBURN

I must get home,
my chocolate needs me.

There are no shortcuts to any place worth going.

BEVERLY SILLS

You are the reason
to share my chocolate.

Treat everybody like it's
their birthday.

True love is giving her the last piece of chocolate.

I can resist everything
except temptation.

OSCAR WILDE

If I had to live my life again, I'd make the same mistakes, only sooner.

TALLULAH BANKHEAD

Everyone must believe in something. I believe I will have another chocolate.

On the eighth day,
God created chocolate.

If there's no chocolate in Heaven, I'm not going.

JANE SEABROOK

Notes

Ideas

Plans

Notes

Thoughts

Ideas

Schemes

MORE FROM ALLEGRA PUBLICATIONS

The Meaning of Husbands

The Meaning of Coffee

The Meaning of Wine

The Meaning of Meow

The London Coffee Guide

The New York Coffee Guide

The Vienna Coffee Guide

The Belgium & Netherlands Coffee Guide

The London Cheese & Wine Guide

Great Cake Places

Allegra
PUBLICATIONS